HARBOROUGH
in Camera

HARBOROUGH
in Camera

*Victorian Photographs of
the Market Harborough Area*

PAM AUCOTT AND STEPH MASTORIS

ALAN SUTTON
LEICESTERSHIRE MUSEUMS, ARTS AND RECORDS SERVICE

First published in the United Kingdom in 1992
Alan Sutton Publishing Ltd · Phoenix Mill · Far Thrupp · Stroud
Gloucestershire

In association with Leicestershire Museums, Arts and Records Service

British Library Cataloguing in Publication Data

Aucott, Pam
  Harborough in Camera: Victorian Photographs of
  the Market Harborough Area
  I. Title II. Mastoris, S.N.
  942.544081

ISBN 0–7509–0283–3

For Terry
chauffeur, typist, critic and friend

Typeset in 11/14 Palatino.
Typesetting and origination by
Alan Sutton Publishing Limited.
Printed in Great Britain by
Butler & Tanner Ltd, Frome and London

CONTENTS

ACKNOWLEDGEMENTS   6

INTRODUCTION   7

Section One   THE PHOTOGRAPHIC
                PROCESSES   11

Section Two   THE PHOTOGRAPHERS   30

Section Three   THE PHOTOGRAPHS   66

ACKNOWLEDGEMENTS

As always with books of this nature many people have provided help, advice and assistance. The greatest debt is obviously to the many generous people who have shared their photographs with us by either donating or loaning them for copying. The names of as many of these as can be traced are listed on page 160.

Special thanks must also go to Steve Thursfield and Catherine Lines of the Photographic Section of Leicestershire Museums for copying literally hundreds of early photographs, their efforts often resulting in a clearer image than the original.

Colleagues at the Harborough Museum – staff and volunteers – have provided essential support by processing and documenting the ever growing photo collection. Thanks are due, in particular, to Janet Alderson-Smith, Kate Brown, John Carter, Norman Davey, Sue Grant, Derek Ingleby and Susan Stretton.

Very grateful thanks go to Northamptonshire Record Office and Northamptonshire Libraries for allowing access to items in their collections.

Leicestershire Museums, Arts and Records Service is always keen to acquire or copy other historic photographs relating to the area covered by this book, and indeed the rest of the county.

INTRODUCTION

This book contains most, and certainly the best, of the topographical photographs taken in and around the town of Market Harborough before the end of the nineteenth century. These are discussed in the context of the development of photography in the area, and the biographies of the people who created the images.

Market Harborough is a classic example of the small country towns of 'middle England'. Following its foundation as a planned commercial centre in the twelfth century, Market Harborough has proved to be an enduring settlement. For at least the last 500 years it has provided the economic centre of gravity in southeast Leicestershire and for twenty or so villages across the River Welland in Northamptonshire.

It is therefore not surprising that photographically this area's topography and population should have been recorded during the first sixty years of the process. However, even the casual reader of this book will soon appreciate the exceptional quantity and quality of photographs taken here and the fine heritage of historic images which has survived. This seems to be the result of several factors.

Many of the earliest photographs of the area are the legacy of two enthusiastic and gifted amateurs. If the Revd William Law had not chosen to spend sixty-three years of his clerical career as rector of Marston Trussell and if William John Jennings had not lived in Little

Bowden for about twenty years most villages in the surrounding area would not be represented in this book at all.

Another factor contributing to the wealth of the area's photographic heritage was its proximity to the Victorian main line railway between the Midlands and London. Leicester was connected to London and Birmingham via Rugby in 1840, and Market Harborough had similar indirect access a decade later. By 1857 the town was connected directly to London along the Midland Railway. This would have enabled photographic equipment and materials to be readily available locally, and bulky and delicate cameras (together with portable darkrooms) to be transported around the area. The railway also provided employment for one of the local photographers (William Jennings) and made it possible for another (George Albert Nichols) to establish a branch studio in Market Harborough while living in Stamford.

The railway was important to the continued prosperity of the area in the second half of the nineteenth century. No longer did Market Harborough service just the agricultural economy of the rich Welland Valley grazing lands. By the 1870s the town could boast burgeoning manufacturing industries – coffee milling, corsets, hosiery, rubber goods and printing equipment – all relying on rail transport for raw materials and the distribution of finished products. These businesses created wealth generally, but in particular gave rise to a small middle class of skilled artisans to complement the traditional small independent shopkeeper as the leaven of local society. These were the people who provided a large enough clientele to support at least one photographic portrait studio in the town from the 1860s onwards.

The final reason for the quantity of Victorian photographs lies with their physical survival, and this is due largely to the museum provision in the town from the 1930s. Over three-quarters of the images here are to be found in the collection of the Harborough Museum. This was established as a branch of the Leicestershire Museums, Arts and Records Service in 1982, but the origins of its collections lie with the foundation of the Market Harborough Historical and Archaeological Society in 1931. Very soon after this group's establishment its members began amassing local antiquities, manuscripts and photographs, and these form the heart of the present collection. However, this has been greatly extended as a result of a decade of active curatorial work by the museum's staff, many images being archival copy prints from historic items on short term loan to the museum. This collection programme continues, but the number of nineteenth-century photographs coming to light has declined to a small trickle. It therefore seems an appropriate time to take stock of the collection, compare it with similar items in other repositories and produce a fairly definitive anthology. These are among the aims of this book.

Section One provides a brief guide to the early photographic processes and their local practitioners. The images reproduced here have been limited to photographs taken before 1900, since after this date cheaper and simpler photographic processes and cameras became widespread. The new century also witnessed a radical change in the format of photographs and the people creating them, as close behind these technological developments came the rapid growth of the picture postcard industry.

Privately printed postcards for use with adhesive stamps were first allowed by the Post Office in 1894, but regulations restricted picture and message to one side of the card leaving the other side for the address. In 1898 these regulations were relaxed, and changes to the permitted size of cards in 1899 created the picture postcard we know today. Soon large numbers of people were sending and collecting cards covering a diversity of subjects. Local photographers as well as national postcard publishers were producing scenic postcards and almost every village had its own set of views. As a result, between 1900 and 1910 far more local topographical images were produced than during any decade in the nineteenth century. Also, photography was no longer the preserve of the wealthy, skilled amateur and the professional.

A study of all the known Victorian photographs of the area shows that 75 per cent can be attributed to six people, two amateurs and four professionals. A further six professionals with studios in the area were responsible for most of the rest. In addition, four other professionals are known solely from entries in contemporary commercial directories. With so few practitioners, it is both possible and relevant to give brief biographies of each so as to provide a full picture of photographic activity in the Harborough area. These form Section Two of the book.

Section Three is devoted to a tour around the Harborough area through the camera lenses of these photographers. This area extends from Kibworth in the north to Kelmarsh in the south, and from Naseby and the Kilworths in the west to Weston by Welland and Wilbarston in the east.

Section One

THE PHOTOGRAPHIC PROCESSES

The birth of photography in 1839 made it possible to capture an image in complete detail for all time. Locally, images survive which date from 1855. Initially portraiture aroused the greatest interest, but the potential for recording places and events was quickly recognized. At first these images concentrated on buildings and included only a few carefully posed people, but by the end of the nineteenth century scenes of crowded streets were not out of the ordinary.

A brief account of the main techniques used in this period is important to understand the constraints under which the photographers laboured and provides a sense of perspective on the development of their work. It is important to remember, however, that these photographers were constantly experimenting and developing their own processing techniques.

The First Photographs

The earliest photographs were made in 1839 using two different processes. In France Louis Daguerre introduced the so-called daguerreotype, and in England William Fox-Talbot created the talbotype or calotype.

Daguerreotypes

The daguerreotype process was used widely in the 1840s and 1850s for professional portraiture. This process was complex but, very briefly, a highly polished silver-coated copper plate was exposed in the camera for between thirty and sixty seconds. Bright sunlight was essential and sitters for portraits were often placed in a head clamp to prevent movement during the exposure time. After exposure the image was 'set' on the plate by suspending it over warmed mercury. To protect the image from damage it was usually sealed in a glass-fronted mount.

Although photographs produced by this process were very fine in detail there were major drawbacks. The exposed plate was developed to become the finished photograph, so no copies could be made. The image produced was also reversed from left to right, and the reflective quality of the plate itself required that it was placed at a right angle to the light for the image to be seen clearly. Daguerreotypes were also expensive The complexities of the process left it largely in the hands of the professional and the limitations led to its demise by the mid-1850s.

The quality of the image from a daguerreotype can be seen in plate 1. This example was found among the

Plate 1: Daguerreotype of an unidentified village, probably in the Harborough area, 1856. (? W. Law) [NRO MaT 206]

effects of the Law family in Marston Trussell rectory and was probably taken by William Law himself. Unfortunately, the village depicted has not yet been identified. No other local photographer is known to have used the daguerreotype process.

Calotypes and Waxed Paper Negatives

The calotype process of Fox-Talbot used good quality writing paper coated with potassium iodide and silver nitrate solutions. The coated paper was then exposed in the camera to produce a negative image, taking between ten seconds and two minutes for a portrait, and between one and five minutes for a landscape. The image was then 'set' using applications of gallic acid and silver nitrate solution. A layer of wax was often applied to these paper negatives to facilitate printing. A modification to the waxing process was introduced in 1851 by Gustav le Gray, who found that waxing the paper before sensitizing increased the length of time it could be stored prior to exposure from twenty-four hours to several weeks. He also found that this improved the detail recorded on the negative.

Once 'set', or developed, the negative could be used to make paper prints. Fox-Talbot produced a printing paper treated with salt and silver nitrate solutions, but the image tended to fade badly. These 'salted' paper prints were superseded by albumen prints introduced by L.D. Blanquard-Everard. These remained in use until the end of the nineteenth century. Albumen printing paper was produced by coating the paper with egg white. The thickness of the coating determined the finish of the print, the thicker the coating the higher the gloss on the print.

Prints were produced by placing the prepared paper and the negative together in sunlight in a printing frame, until an image was imprinted on the paper. It could take anything from several minutes to several hours to make each print. The imprinted image was then 'set' in the same way as the negative image. The printing paper itself was usually thin and liable to curl at the edges, so most photographs were pasted on to card to prevent this occurring.

Complications arising from the laws of patent made this process more attractive to the amateur than the professional. Like the daguerreotype, the calotype and its derivatives were little used after the 1850s.

LIFE IN PORTRAITURE:

MR. WHITLOCK most respectfully announces that his Stay in Northampton is limited to a very short period, and calls attention to the fact that

THE INIMITABLE

PHOTOGRAPHIC PORTRAITS,

(By Beard's Patent Process)

ARE REDUCED TO HALF THE LONDON CHARGES,

AT THE

PHOTOGRAPHIC ROOMS,

MERCERS' ROW, NORTHAMPTON.

Price of Small Busts, 10s. 6d. Portraits, Lockets, Brooches, &c., on the same reduced scale.

A variety of Cases from 2s. and upwards.

PHOTOGRAPHIC PORTRAITS.

BROWN & HEWITT,

BOOKSELLERS, &c. BIBLE AND CROWN, MARKET-PLACE, LEICESTER.

BEG to announce that they have purchased of the proprietor, the Patent Right for taking those wonderful productions PHOTOGRAPHIC PORTRAITS, and VIEWS, &c. which, after a considerable outlay, they are now prepared to do on their premises.

This astonishing discovery being generally known, it is not necessary to dwell upon the process by which these beautiful and faithful pictures are produced. Without affecting in the slightest degree to depreciate the excellence of art, it is due to this new feature of science, to assert its immense superiority in the quick and certain accomplishment of all that it professes to aim at.

The consideration of two or three points will convince us of this.—We all crave the possession of portraits—of ourselves for others, of others for ourselves. Now, in sitting for a picture, the essential stipulation is, that it should be *like*. The one charm and merit of a portrait, must consist in its being a *likeness*. Some of us may possibly stipulate for a slight touch of flattery, just the lightest in the world, but, generally, we prefer truth when we can get it; often in our own case—and always in the case of others. A Parent, a Child, a Wife, — Friend, we wish to have them painted "to the Life." The feeling that inspires the wish is too sacred to be trifled with by the flattery of the painter. We desire no fiction but the exact semblance of reality.

Here then is a grand advantage in the Photographic Art; the *facsimile* is produced. The chances of mistake are precluded.—There before you is the sitter, in his habit as he lives, and he equally lives in this beautiful reflection. It is his own image, as true to him as his shadow is. Such a portrait of the absent, or of the dead, held in remembrance of any object of our regard or love, must be invaluable; it will be dearer from its perfect freedom from flattery, it will be prized because it is identity itself—And this wonderful effect is produced in one minute! and the annoyance of tedious "Sittings for one's picture" done away with.

PORTRAITS TAKEN DAILY,

At the Bible and Crown, Market-place, Leicester,

WHERE A GREAT VARIETY OF SPECIMENS MAY BE SEEN.

It being a very general opinion that Photographic portraits can only be taken when the sun shines, B. & H. beg to say that cloudy weather is equally favourable to the operation.

Early Professional Applications

The potential of photography as a commercial enterprise was recognized from its earliest days, with the first London studio opening in 1841. In 1844 studios were opened by a Mr Whitlock in Northampton, and in Leicester by Thomas Chapman Brown, a printer and stationer. These early establishments concentrated on portraiture using the daguerreotype process.

It soon became fashionable to have a daguerreotype likeness made, and although a much larger proportion of the population could afford a daguerreotype as opposed to a painted miniature they were not cheap. In 1845 Mr Whitlock advertised his prices as being half the London charges with small busts costing 10s. 6d. and carrying cases from 2s. By 1855, at the very end of the daguerreotype era, a Leicester photographer, J. Eastham, was offering daguerreotypes for 4s. unframed and 5s. framed. This was still a great deal of money at a time when an agricultural worker could only expect to earn 8s. to 9s. per week and a domestic servant £10 to £12 per year. So the photograph remained out of the reach of many and Market Harborough, with a population of under 2,500 in 1851, could not sustain a professional daguerreotypist.

It is interesting to note that, although photography would have been a very expensive hobby, it was possible to obtain the necessary materials in both Leicester and Northampton at certain chemists specializing in photographic requisites: Thomas Parsons in Leicester (*Leicester Journal*, 1 April 1859) and William Harris in Northampton (*Northampton Mercury*, 6 September 1856).

Later Processes and the Spread of Photography
The Wet Collodion Process

In 1851 Frederick Archer introduced the wet collodion process, which utilized a glass plate coated with collodion. This was a sticky liquid made from guncotton (nitrate of potash, sulphuric acid and cotton) dissolved in ether and then mixed with potassium iodide. To be effective the plate had to be sensitized by immersion in a solution of silver nitrate, exposed immediately, and developed in the twenty minutes before the plate dried.

Initially there was no overall concensus that this was a superior process and experimentation continued, in particular with attempts to find a satisfactory 'manipulation' (process) using dry plates. William Law was using dry plates from at least 1856. However, by 1860 wet collodion plates had superseded both calotypes and daguerreotypes, and this remained the most commonly used process for the next twenty years.

This technique overcame the major disadvantages of the two earlier processes. Unlike calotypes, wet collodion plates gave negatives which were finer in detail and less prone to fading. Unlike daguerreotypes, they allowed an unlimited number of copies to be made. Printing was also speeded up because a negative of glass was now used, although it still remained a time consuming procedure. Most professional photographers employed an apprentice to help with printing.

Perhaps the greatest advantage of this new technique was cost, in that at least two paper prints could be obtained for the price previously paid for a single daguerreotype. (See the advertisement of J.Burton and Sons in the *Leicester Journal* of 1 April 1859 on p. 17.) As a result, professional photography became more widespread, and this can be seen in the number of studios operating in Leicester by the 1860s. The commercial directories record only one studio working in the 1840s and two opened during the 1850s. During the 1860s, however, there were about a dozen operating at any one time (B.V. & P.F. Heathcote, *Leicester Photographic Studios in Victorian and Edwardian Times*).

The earliest local exponents of the collodion process were both amateurs – William Law and William John Jennings – but it is not known whether these two gentlemen met or collaborated in their photographic work.

The Carte-de-visite

The use of wet collodion processes led to a greater diversification in subject matter, with landscapes becoming increasingly popular. It also brought about the carte-de-visite photograph. These were so called because they were the same size as visiting cards. It soon became fashionable to collect these photographic cards, many of which were mass-produced and covered a wide range of subjects. However, they also gave local photographers a new outlet for their work and many produced views of towns and major buildings in their area.

The carte-de-visite had been made possible through the work of a French portrait photographer, Adolphe

Plate 2: A carte-de-visite of an unidentified man, late 1860s. (J. P. Jennings) [LEIMH 100.1983.1353]

Disderi. In 1854 he devised a camera with four lenses, each exposing only a quarter section of half a large plate. When this had been exposed the plate was moved over so that the other half could also be exposed. This format reduced the cost of a photograph once again. A set of ten cartes cost 10s. in Leicester during the 1860s, and this compared very favourably with the two guineas which was often charged for a single large photograph (advertisement of John Burton and Sons in Buchanan's *Leicestershire Directory* for 1867).

The prints were mounted on stiff card, the reverse of which was usually embellished with the photographer's name and address. These small photographs were often given as mementos to the sitter's family and friends. Plate 2 shows an example of a carte-de-visite produced in Market Harborough in the late 1860s at about its actual size. The man is seated in a traditional studio pose and setting.

It was during the early years of the wet plate era that the first professional studio was opened in Market Harborough by John Payne Jennings. This was located in a room at No. 5 High Street. All the photographs known to have come from this studio were in the carte-de-visite format, perhaps reflecting the importance of cost to the viability of a photographic studio in a small town. Surviving photographs suggest that the clientele of this establishment were tradespeople and farmers from the town and surrounding villages.

In 1866 the 'cabinet' size print was introduced. This was double the size of the carte-de-visite and presented in much the same way, with the image pasted onto a card mount which advertised the photographer on the back. In 1867 J. & T. Spencer of Leicester offered these at

26

5s. for the first copy, with further copies available at 1s. 6d. each (Buchanan's *Leicestershire Directory* for 1867).

It now became possible to obtain further copies of photographs by post. An advertisement bearing a London address appeared in the *Market Harborough Advertiser* of February 1872 offering a set of twelve cartes-de-visite from the sender's original for 2s. 8d. Copies obtained by this means were cheaper than those from the local photographers. However, costs generally continued to fall, and by the mid-1870s cartes were available locally from 5s. a dozen (advertisement of Byron & Clayton in the *Leicester Advertiser*, 7 February 1875).

The Dry Plate

Further technical advances were made during the 1870s. In 1871 Richard Maddox discovered that by using gelatine instead of collodion to coat the glass plates it was no longer necessary to expose and develop them while they were still wet. Also, this new coating was much more light-sensitive, so reducing exposure times to fractions of a second. It was not until 1878 that the process became widely used, and in 1879 commercially produced gelatine dry plates became available. Their uniform coating of the plate helped to produce a better quality print.

The availability of these products simplified taking pictures and outdoor photography especially became much more practical. It was no longer essential to learn the skills needed to prepare the plates. A dark-room, however, was still required to develop those which had been exposed.

Gelatine emulsion was also used on printing paper – the so-called 'bromide' paper. This was used as a development paper rather than printing out paper. It was exposed against the negative for a few seconds and then the image was brought out chemically before being fixed, rather than being exposed against the negative until the image reached the required intensity for fixing. Time spent on print making was consequently reduced.

The increased sensitivity of this paper also meant that it was possible to make enlargements using artificial light. Previously, only sunlight had been strong enough for this, and a dark-room required an opening through which the sun's rays could pass. In practice, enlarging was seldom carried out before this new paper became available.

These new developments gave much greater scope to the photographer, changing the emphasis from places to particular events or activities and what may be called 'action' photographs. It also allowed the macabre practice of the time of photographing the corpses of loved ones who had died.

By this time cost seems to have become a less significant factor in the selling of photographs and few advertisements make any reference to prices. However, an advertisement of F.W. Broadhead in Wright's *Leicestershire Directory* for 1886 suggests that these advances in technology had in fact had little effect on the cost of a photograph. He was charging 5s. for a dozen cartes-de-visite – the same price they had been a decade earlier.

An interesting advertisement appeared in the *Market Harborough Advertiser* in September 1884 offering carte-de-visite photographs of the old railway station at 6d. each (the new station had just been opened). Two larger format photographs of the old railway station survive, which were taken in about 1883 by George Nichols (plates 3 and 4). It is possible that the same images were used for the photographs advertised.

Under the Patronage of their
Royal Highnesses

The Prince and Princess
of Wales.

F. W. BROADHEAD,
ARTIST PHOTOGRAPHER.

*CARTE DE VISITES from 5/- per Dozen. The new CARTE MIDGET
from 2/- per Dozen.*

Portraits enlarged and copied, and finished as Oil Paintings, Water Colour Drawings, or Plain Photographs. Photographs by Artificial Light during Winter Months. Out-door Photography in all its branches. Groups and Residences photographed by arrangement. Terms on application to

F. W. BROADHEAD, 65, WELFORD ROAD, LEICESTER.
AND 5, HIGH STREET, MARKET HARBORO'.

Alongside the continuing use of the carte-de-visite and cabinet print there was an increasing demand for larger format photographs, especially for groups and topographical subjects. These are often found pasted onto even larger pieces of card, presumably ready for framing.

Plate 3: Railway staff outside the first station at Market Harborough, 1883.
(G.A. Nichols) [LEIMH 100.1983.1428]

Plate 4: The platforms of the Market Harborough railway station, 1883.
(G.A. Nichols) [LEIMH 92.1983.43]

Photography for All

From the 1850s changes began to occur in national working practices and there was an increase in real wages for both skilled and unskilled. The growth of trade unionism led to a reduction in the working week, and a Saturday half day was also becoming standard in most organized trades. These changes gave people more money to spend and also more time in which to pursue interests such as photography.

The effect of short exposure times and the practicality of making enlargements had important implications for camera design. Now that it was no longer necessary to have a large plate for contact printing or long exposure times the camera could be much smaller. The use of a mechanical shutter was also better suited to short exposure times (1/25 of a second), and this provided yet another simplification of the photographic process. These developments in cameras, together with commercially prepared plates and chemicals, took much of the uncertainty out of taking photographs.

The final obstacles to amateur photography were removed by the work of George Eastman of America. In 1884 he introduced gelatine-coated paper negatives as an alternative to glass plates, and in 1889 these were replaced by cellulose nitrate to create the transparent flexible negative used in a roll form which we know today. The great advantage of this was that the roll of film could be placed in the camera and several photographs taken before it was removed for developing.

By the end of 1889 Eastman had produced the first 'Kodak' camera, specifically designed for the amateur. This camera was sold complete with film of 100 exposures. It worked with a simple push button action.

When the entire film had been exposed the camera was returned to the factory for the film to be developed and printed, and a new film was loaded in the camera. This was the first example of commercial processing and it made it unnecessary for the amateur to have his or her own dark-room, or indeed to have any knowledge of the technical side of photography. Their sole interest could be in the finished product.

At a cost of five guineas, however, this camera was still expensive. The introduction of the first 'Brownie' box camera in 1900 at a price of 5s. overcame the final barrier of expense. Photography was no longer restricted to the dedicated few but was available to all.

The impact of these changes began to be seen in the latter years of the nineteenth century. As early as 1894 the number of local enthusiasts must have been increasing as Green's the chemists at No. 2 High Street, Market Harborough found it worthwhile to stock photographic requisites (*Market Harborough Advertiser*, 31 July 1894).

UNDER THE PATRONAGE OF

Their Royal Highnesses
the Prince and Princess of Wales, His Grace the Duke of Rutland, K.G.,

AND THE NOBILITY AND GENTRY OF THE COUNTY.

F. W. BROADHEAD,
𝕬rtist 𝕻hotographer.

CARTES-DE-VISITE FROM 5/- PER DOZ.   CABINETS FROM 14/- PER DOZ.

Portraits enlarged and copied, and finished as Oil Paintings, Water Colour Drawings, or Plain Photographs.   Photographs by Artificial Light during Winter Months.   Out-door Photography in all its branches.   Groups and Residences photographed by arrangement. Terms and Pamphlet of Testimonials on application to

F. W. BROADHEAD, 55, WELFORD ROAD, LEICESTER,
AND 5, HIGH STREET, MARKET HARBOROUGH.

THE CENTRAL PHARMACY.

E. GREEN,

CHEMIST, MARKET HARBOROUGH.

THE CHEAPEST SHOP IN THE TOWN FOR PATENT AND
PROPRIETARY MEDICINES FOR CASH.

SEIGEL'S 1s. BEECHAM'S PILLS 7d. AND 9½d.

MEDICINES FRESH FROM LONDON DAILY.

THE only Establishment in Harborough where a PHARMACEUTICAL CHEMIST is at the Service or Customers. All Prescriptions dispensed with the PUREST DRUGS, PERSONALLY, by a qualified Pharmacist of West-end of London experience, at Store prices. Analyses undertaken. Photographic requisites in Stock or to order. GREEN'S noted Ginger Beer 1/6 per doz, and Ginger Beer Powder 3d per packet. Powder for Tender Feet 6d. per box, trial packet, 3d. GREEN'S Nursery Hair Lotion, 6d. and 1/- per bottle. The Noted Dorking Lavender Water as prepared from a recipe as formerly supplied to the Queen. Bottles 1s., 1/9, 8/-

2, High-street, Market Harborough.

Although it is impossible to know how many amateur photographers there were locally, a competition sponsored by the *Market Harborough Advertiser* to depict celebrations for Edward VII's coronation in 1902 suggests they were numerous. Despite the wider use of photography the professional continued to prosper. In the first decade of the twentieth century six individuals described themselves as 'photographer' in local commercial directories. Another two seem to have had some income from photography. One of these was William Cort, a boot and shoe manufacturer from Church Street, Market Harborough. He ran a camera hire service from around 1905 and took the photographs published in the supplement to the *Market Harborough Advertiser* which commemorated the opening of the new cattle market in 1903. Others such as F.C. Hawke, the postmaster at Hallaton, took photographs which they then published in postcard form. Overall, the era of mass photography had arrived and more and more photographs of people, places and events were being taken.

THE PHOTOGRAPHERS

Reverend William Law

The earliest known amateur photographer in the area was the Reverend William Law of Marston Trussell. Over 250 of his photographs have survived, spanning a period of more than thirty years. William Law was born in 1812 in Gawcott, Buckinghamshire, the son of a prosperous farmer. In 1831 he went to Queen's College, Cambridge, graduating in 1837 (according to Christine Allington, William Law's great granddaughter). The following year he took up his first living at Great Linford in Buckinghamshire. By the end of 1842 he had bought the living at Marston Trussell and he remained rector there until his death in 1900. In 1846 he built The Coombes, an imposing brick house perched high on the southern escarpment of the Welland Valley, nearer to Sibbertoft than his own parish. This house and its grounds feature prominently in many of his photographs.

Law's interest in photography spanned several changes in technique, beginning with daguerreotypes and proceeding to experimentation with paper negatives and both wet and dry collodion plates. The bulk of Law's surviving work constitutes some 200 waxed paper negatives, dating between 1855 and 1856. There are many slight variations in the sizes of these negatives

Plate 5: Marston Trussell church, 1855. (W. Law) [LEIMH 100.1983.2495]

but, in general, it seems he used up to five different cameras. Technical notes appear in the corner of some of the negatives.

An example is seen in plate 5, where a note on the left hand side of the print records that it was taken on 5 May 1855 at 11.15 a.m., using an eight minute exposure. Notes on the right hand side indicate the paper was produced by Marion & Co. and had been waxed.

Of the 200 paper negatives, 140 depict his house and grounds, 12 are portraits, and 49 topographical. However, only eighteen of these topographical photographs come from the immediate locality. Of these, ten depict local churches and two Marston Trussell Hall. Five of the remainder show Market Harborough, although three of these show the same view up the High Street, differing only in detail. Only one other local topographical negative has survived and this shows Naseby.

From the mid-1850s Law was also experimenting with collodion and developed a dry plate process. Unfortunately, no glass plates survive but seventy-nine prints from them are known. These are mostly family portraits, some using the carte-de-visite format, and landscape views of The Coombes gardens, with a few depicting local villages. As with the waxed paper negatives, there are many slight variations in the size of these prints, although the majority were taken with half- and quarter-plate cameras. The latest dated print from a collodion plate shows Marston Trussell in 1875 (plate 6). However, Law continued to take an active interest in photography until his death, and in the 1890s he made many prints from earlier plates.

Plate 6: Looking west along Main Street, Marston Trussell, 1875. (W. Law) [LEIMH 100.1983.2151]

William Law is known to have had a wide interest in things scientific and this is reflected in his photography. Through continual experimentation with variations in the techniques he used, he seems not only to be attempting to improve the quality of his photographs but also to research into optics and chemistry. Although Law's interest was technical rather than artistic, his photographs are very well composed.

William John Jennings

The second of the early amateur photographers of the Harborough area was William John Jennings. He was born in Plymouth, Devon in about 1819. At the time of the census in 1841 he lived in Gayton, a village near Northampton, and was employed as a plate layer on the railway. He later moved to Great Oakhamstead, Hertfordshire. By the time he came to Harborough in the 1850s he had risen to the position of permanent way inspector with the Midland Railway Company with a salary of some £2–£3 per week.

After moving to Harborough, Jennings built a substantial house, The Chestnuts on Kettering Road. Perhaps he had inherited some money as his income would not appear to have been sufficient for this. The Chestnuts remained his home until about 1880, when he moved to Ashtead, Epsom, Surrey.

Jennings' greatest interest in his photography seems to have been in church architecture. The photograph of Great Easton church with figures in the foreground on p. 34 is typical of his work.

This interest brought him into contact with the Architectural Society of the Archdeaconry of Northampton (later the Northamptonshire Archaeological Society).

Plate 7: The chancel and north side of Great Easton church, about 1860. (W.J. Jennings) [NRO: NAS 48/27]

One of the aims of this society was to 'procure photo-graphic pictures of all old buildings of any architec-tural character before they are destroyed or restored'. By August 1859 he had been 'engaged to work for the society on the most reasonable terms', charging 7s. 6d. for the first full-sized view and 3s. 6d. for sub-sequent copies. In the following year he was commis-sioned to 'obtain faithful representations of all the ancient bridges on the Nene and other rivers in the county'.

The Northamptonshire Record Office now holds the archives of the society and this includes more than fifty church photographs taken by Jennings. These con-centrate on the villages along the southern boundary of the Welland Valley, in an area extending from Caldecot and Rockingham in the east to Theddingworth and Naseby in the west. Smaller groups of photographs also survive for Northampton and around the Northamptonshire-Bedfordshire border.

Ten photographs of the Harborough area survive, providing street scenes of Market Harborough, Great Bowden and Lubenham. Jennings' photographs appear to have been produced using the wet collodion process. As the plates used in this process need to be developed in the twenty minutes before the coating dries, Jennings, in addition to his plate camera and tri-pod, must have had a portable dark-room. This was a cumbersome piece of apparatus incorporating a tent, the glass plates, and all the chemicals necessary for preparing and developing the plates. A supply of clean water was also needed.

An examination of Jennings' photographs reveals prints of three different sizes, suggesting the use of at least three different cameras (enlargements were seldom

Plate 8: Looking north up the High Street, Market Harborough, between 1859 and 1863. (? W.J. Jennings) [LEIMH 51.1989.27]

attempted at this time because of the problem of inade-quate lighting). Jennings seems to have taken great pains with the composition of his photographs, many incorpo-rating figures posed informally to provide a focal point for the foreground. However, apart from the posed fig-ures, the streets show little sign of life or other activity.

John Payne Jennings

The first professional photographer known to have worked in the area was John Payne Jennings, the son of William John Jennings. The census returns for 1861 show that John Payne Jennings was 18 years old, lived with his parents at The Chestnuts, and worked as a photographic artist. He was born at Gayton, a village near Northampton, which was also his mother's birth-place.

In April 1861 William Jennings bought the premises at No. 5 High Street and it was here that the first studio was located. It is not known whether the studio was rented prior to the purchase of the property. Plate 8 is the only early photograph to include No. 5 High Street and was taken between 1859 and 1863. During 1863 and 1864 Jennings operated a lending library and read-ing room from the premises (*Midland Free Press*, 6 July 1863). Part of the building was later let for retail use, Joseph Healey, a tailor, advertising his business there in 1866. (*Midland Free Press*, 1866).

All the photographs directly attributable to John Payne Jennings use the carte-de-visite format so pop-ular in the early 1860s. His description of himself as a 'photographic artist' is soon appreciated on a close inspection of his townscapes. As with his father's work, composition is an important element. The

Plate 9: The east side of the upper High Street, Market Harborough, between 1864 and 1869. (J.P. Jennings) [LEIMH 100.1983.1355]

photographs appear to fall into two separate categories: general views and specific buildings. This may reflect two different aspects of his work: speculative views for general sale and commissions for particular customers. Plate 9, showing Nos 45–51 High Street, is typical of his general street scenes. His compositional touch is seen in the delivery boy standing in the road.

Almost all the surviving photographs by J.P. Jennings depict Harborough, although views of Rockingham Castle and Holdenby House are known suggesting that he did work in a much wider area. It may be that these are just two in a series of photographs of large buildings offered for sale by Jennings.

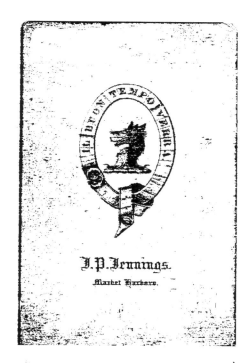

PHOTOGRAPHED BY
J. P. JENNINGS
MARKET HARBORO'.

No.

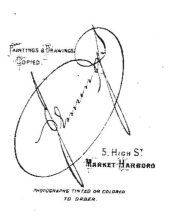

John Payne Jennings continued to take photographs until about 1870. It is not known what happened to him after this date, but no later examples of his work appear and his name disappears from the local commercial directories.

Jennings used five different designs for the backs of his cartes-de-visite. Unfortunately, it is not possible to verify the order in which they were used. The simplest was probably the earliest, which was followed by the family crest of a wolf's head surrounded by a garter containing a motto, *il buon tempo verra* ('he sees good times'). The remaining three designs bear the name 'Jennings' only and no initials, and this may reflect a change in the running of the business, either to a partnership with Susan Jennings or a complete takeover by her.

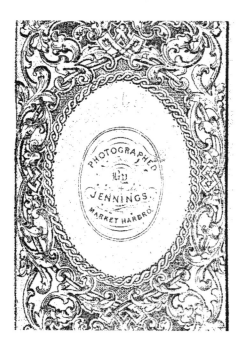
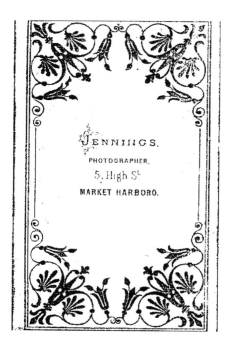

Susan Jennings

Susan Jennings was born in Weymouth, Dorset in the early 1830s, and in the 1861 census returns for Little Bowden she was already recorded as a widow. She was the sister-in-law of William Jennings and until 1872 lived with his family.

Her known association with photography begins in March of 1870 when she advertised the reopening of the photographic rooms at No. 5 High Street (*Market Harborough Advertiser*, 22 March 1870). It is not known how long they had been closed prior to this reopening. William's wife had died on 5 March and this may have called a temporary halt to business, but the fact that Susan also advertised for an assistant may indicate a longer closure. It is interesting to note that Susan felt a training in photography was sufficient recompense for an assistant and did not offer to pay a salary.

In February 1872 she took over the shop at No. 5 High Street, opening a fancy goods repository to be run

PHOTOGRAPHIC ROOMS,
5, HIGH STREET,
MARKET HARBOROUGH.

MRS. JENNINGS begs to notify that she has re-opened her Photographic Studio.

An active and intelligent Youth is required to assist at the above.

A thorough knowledge of the Photographic Art will be taught him, in return for his services; and a small salary given after the first 12 months.

Apply between 11 and 2, as above.

Plate 10: The east side of Church Square, Market Harborough, between 1877 and 1879. (? Susan Jennings) [LEIMH 99.1987.303]

in conjunction with the photographic business (*Market Harborough Advertiser*, 20 February 1872). The photographic rooms were located at the back of the building on the first floor with access from an external staircase. The fancy goods business gradually became predominant, and although in White's *Leicestershire Directory* of 1877 she is still listed as a photographer by 1880 the studio had been sublet. Susan continued in business in the town until her death in March 1912. Her obituary appears in the *Market Harborough Advertiser* for 19 March 1912.

None of the surviving photographs of the Harborough area can be attributed to Susan with any certainty. Some of the cartes-de-visite which bear the name 'Jennings' with no initial could be the product of a partnership between John Payne and Susan, or Susan's work alone. One other 'unsigned' photograph is probably her work (plate 10). This dates from the late 1870s and contrasts sharply in style with the work of E.H. Speight, the only other photographer of Market Harborough at this time.

Edward Hall Speight

Although not a photographer based in Market Harborough, a brief review of E.H. Speight's work is included because he did produce a series of photographs of the town in the late 1870s.

Census returns for Rugby show that Edward Hall Speight was born in Ambleside, Westmorland in about 1835. The first reference to him living in the Midlands is in 1862 when he was the Wesleyan schoolmaster at New Bilton (now part of Rugby). In Kenning's Directory of Rugby for 1870 Speight is recorded as being at the Wesleyan school in Chapel Street, Rugby, but he is also described as a photographer working from his home address at No. 16 Lawford Road. The commercial directory published four years later still lists him as the schoolmaster but also carries an advertisement for the photographic business. This appears to have been concerned mainly with portraiture.

What seems to have begun as a hobby finally became a full-time occupation in 1875 when he gave up the position of schoolmaster and moved to No. 35 Dunchurch Road. An advertisement in 1877 shows that now he was a professional photographer he had widened his range of subjects to include landscape photography.

Speight's photographs of Market Harborough date from the late 1870s. They represent the largest group of topographical photographs of the town at this date. Their very existence suggests that there was no local photographer to undertake this kind of work. All the photographs are in the carte-de-visite format and show a marked contrast in style to the Jennings views of a decade earlier. The photograph showing the former Little Bowden police station on Northampton Road is

typical of his approach (plate 11). While Jennings near-
ly always included people, in Speight's work figures
only seem to appear by chance. This is obvious in the
picture looking west along St Mary's Road (plate 12),
where no attempt has been made to bring the group on
the left hand side into focus.

From the probable date of these photographs, it is
likely Speight was using the wet collodion process, in
which case he would have used a portable dark-room.

The 1881 census shows that Speight was already
employing his eldest daughter and two of his sons in a
family business. He remained at No. 35 Dunchurch
Road until the early 1890s, when he moved to No. 16.
The business continued at this address until 1936 when
it finally closed.

Plate 11: The former police station, east side of Northampton Road, Little
Bowden, about 1880. (E.H. Speight) [LEIMH 100.1983.1099]

Plate 12: Looking west along St Mary's Road, at the junction with Mill Hill Road, between 1877 and 1879. (E.H. Speight) [LEIMH 100.1983.1102]

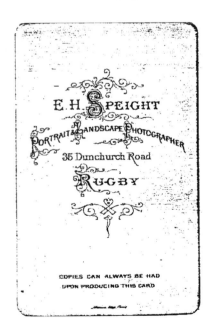

Frederick William Broadhead

Little is known of Frederick William Broadhead's early background except that he was born in London in about 1847 and was still single when he opened his first Leicester studio in about 1870. He described himself as an artist, and machinery and landscape photographer. By 1880 he had extended his business to Harborough on market days. He rented the studio at No. 5 High Street from Susan Jennings. Business must have been brisk, because in July of 1881 he opened on Fridays as well as Tuesdays (*Market Harborough Advertiser*, 12 July 1881).

Broadhead continued in business at various locations in Leicester and in other towns until the turn of the century (according to unpublished research by Mark Gamble).

His early association with Harborough seems to have ended by 1888, but he took over the studio at No. 5 High Street again in 1894 (*Market Harborough Advertiser*, 12 June 1894). However, he was declared bankrupt in December 1896 and his association with Harborough ceased (*Market Harborough Advertiser*, 29 December 1896).

Only three topographical photographs of the area by Broadhead have so far been found and it seems

PHOTOGRAPHIC ESTABLISHMENT
Mrs. JENNINGS, High Street, Market Harborough

F. W. BROADHEAD

WILL attend every FRIDAY, as well as TUESDAY, as before, at the above Establishment until further notice. All Portraits taken by the new instantaneous process. Out-door Photographs, Landscapes. Groups. &c., taken on the shortest notice on application at his Leicester Establishment, 63, Welford Road, or by letter.

probable that his Market Harborough studio concentrated on portraiture. Broadhead continued with the carte-de-visite format for portrait work, and an advertisement of 1884 shows that he also offered 'cartes midgets' at 2s. per dozen, presumably aimed at the poorer sections of the community.

His early advertisements show that he favoured the use of the patent lambertype and chromatype enlarging and printing processes as opposed to the more commonly used albumen printing. By 1881 he had adopted the procedures associated with the gelatine dry plate.

George Albert Nichols

George Albert Nichols was born in Cambridge in about 1840 and was the son of a bookseller (according to unpublished research by Bill Smith). He is believed to have spent some of his early years in America and served in the American Civil War before returning to England in about 1862. Nothing is known of Nichols' whereabouts after his return to England until he appears in the 1871 census returns, living in Southbridge Lane, Croydon and working as a photographic artist. Other members of his household included one apprentice and five boarders, who are also listed as photographers, but it is unclear whether Nichols was also employing these men.

Later commercial directories show Nichols living in Southbridge Lane in 1872 and 1874. However, a carte-de-visite indicates that he also occupied premises at No. 4 London Road (the railway terminus) and No. 2 Waddon New Road. In 1874 he moved to Wormley in Hertfordshire, remaining only a short time before moving to Hitchin. Here he lived at Croydon House in Station Road. His final move was to Stamford in about 1879.

Nichols' association with Harborough commenced in September 1883, when he opened the town's second photographic studio. This was located in Bridge House which stood on the west side of Northampton Road immediately to the south of the Welland bridge. Here he employed a manager, Frederick Trull, to run the studio. A rail link made the journey between the two towns practical, and Nichols' wife probably ran the Stamford side of the business while he attended Market Harborough. In December 1886 he closed the

Harborough studio, but continued working in Stamford until his death ten years later. After his death Nichols' wife carried on the business for some time.

In Nichols' work there is a greater diversity of subject matter than is found in the earlier photographers' work. An 1892 trade guide for Stamford, *Stamford (1892) Illustrated*, reported that,

> Mr Nichols adopts the instantaneous process of photography, which is so much to be depended upon for catching the correct expression of the sitter. . . . [He] makes a feature of photographing views, including noblemen's seats, churches (exterior and interior) and has copies of negatives he

Plate 13: Bridge House, on the south-west side of the Welland bridge, Northampton Road, Market Harborough, 1960s. [LEIMH 99.1987.600]

has taken all over the country, copies of which he supplies at very reasonable prices.

He also retailed photographic apparatus, ready-made solutions, papers, plates, dishes and general accessories and offered a course of instruction on dark-room procedures for beginners who wished to perfect the art. That Nichols travelled widely taking photographs is illustrated by a carte-de-visite with the Croydon address which depicts a house in Clipston (plate 14).

With Nichols' work there is also much greater variation in the size of photographs, another result of changing techniques. While he continued with the carte-de-visite for portrait work, there are also examples of cabinet size and even larger prints. By Nichols' time general landscape and townscape photographs of earlier decades had gone out of fashion, to be replaced by more specific subjects, be it an individual, a church, a group or an activity. Nichols' picture of a brass band, taken in the 1880s, is the earliest known local example of a group photograph (plate 15). He also produced the first local 'action' photographs at the nearby tannery (plates 16 and 17). Although these attempt to convey events in progress, they had to be very carefully stage managed.

Photography.

G. A. Nichols,

Portrait, Architectural, & Landscape Photographer and Picture Frame Manufacturer,

Rutland Villas, Tinwell Road, Stamford, and Coventry Road, Market Harborough.

BEGS respectfully to inform the Gentry and Inhabitants of Market Harborough and its vicinity that he has opened his studio on the Northampton Road near the bridge, and is prepared to execute in the most accurate, artistic, and very best styles, photographs of every description, and trusts to receive a share of public patronage.

Groups, Children, Animals, &c., taken by the Instantaneous Process.

Plate 14: The Chestnuts, Clipston, early 1870s. (G.A. Nichols) [LEIMH 1.1990.142]

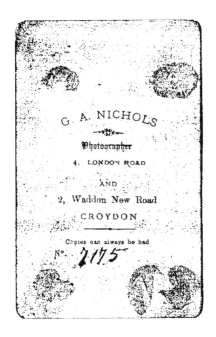

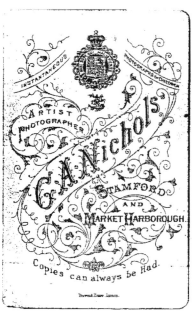

Plate 15: A brass band of the Harborough area, about 1885. (G.A. Nichols)
[LEIMH 100.1983.1401]

Plates 16 and 17: The tannery at work, Market Harborough, about 1885. (? G.A. Nichols) [LEIMH 100.1983. 1190 and 1191]

Gulliver Speight

How well I remember arriving in Market Harborough from a London factory fifty years ago. It was a wet and foggy afternoon. As I walked down the St Mary's Road carrying a gladstone bag and £100 in my pocket, Harborough parish clock struck two. The first building I noticed was an empty flour mill and I sighed to myself 'Oh what have I come to!' . . . The chief events in Market Harborough I found were the April and October Fairs and the Burnaby Shield [shooting] Competition. [The] Tuesday market day was the only day when a good trade was done. Cattle, sheep and pigs were sold at auction in the Square and for the rest of the week Harborough was dead quiet. There was little traffic and, believe it or not, I have seen grass growing in the roadway between Harborough and Kibworth.

(Gulliver Speight, 'My fifty years in Harborough', *Market Harborough Advertiser and Midland Mail*, 1940)

Gulliver Speight was the last of the professional photographers working in the area before 1900. He was born in 1864 at New Bilton, Warwickshire, the eldest son of Edward Hall Speight, the Wesleyan schoolmaster who later became a photographer. By 1881 the census shows that he was already engaged in the family business in Rugby, together with his sister and one of his brothers.

He opened his first studio in Harborough in February 1888 when he was 24 years old and continued this business for more than fifty years (*Market Harborough Advertiser*, 10 January 1888). It is interesting to note that his premises were at No. 5 High Street, the site of the first professional studio in the town. However, by 1894 he had moved to No. 29 The Square and was soon offering a picture framing service. From his advertisements, at least, this would appear to have been of equal importance to photography.

In his autobiographical newspaper article he remembered that 'things went well for me straightaway with receipts first week 7s. 6d.; second £2 19s., and so on. Then came a £30 order from some Americans, who had rented Dingley [Hall] for the season.' Soon after coming to the town he offered 'instantaneous' pictures of the April Fair for sale. A photograph of the fair published in John Bland's book *Bygone Days in Market Harborough* (1924) could well be one of these photographs of 1888, although Bland dates it at 1890 (plate 19). This was the

Plate 18: Gulliver Speight's studio at No. 29 The Square, Market Harborough, about 1915. [LEIMH 41.1986.5]

Plate 19: The April Fair on the Square, Market Harborough, about 1890. (G. Speight) [LEIMH A.6332]

first street scene of the town which had not been specifically posed. The hive of activity on the Square is in marked contrast to the empty streets portrayed in earlier decades. Speight's 1888 advertisement was the only one he made for topographical photographs, for within a few years the picture postcard had cornered this market completely.

Despite the curtailment of demand for topographical photographs for direct sale to the public, Speight did in fact produce a number for use in publications. The *Market Harborough (1892) Illustrated* trade guide printed the earliest local examples of these with its eleven photographs of the town. Five of these were credited to Gulliver Speight, although the style of all the photographs (stiffly posed figures looking directly at the camera) suggests that they were all the work of one person. Only one original of these is known. This shows St Dionysius' church from Church Gate (plate 20). It was taken between February 1888, when Speight came to the town, and December, when Church Gate was demolished for the site of the R. & W.H. Symington factory's 'New Side'.

Plate 20: The south side of Market Harborough parish church, 1888.
(G. Speight) [LEIMH 100.1983.1136]

Portraiture, however, remained popular, and Speight offered cartes-de-visite and cartes midgets as well as larger portraits. However, Speight witnessed the dawning of a new demand for photographs to commemorate specific events. From this time, photographs of sporting and social groups began to appear, and they remain popular to this day (plate 21).

In the fashion of earlier photographers, Gulliver Speight advertised his business on the backs of his early portraits. In later years he changed the presentation of his photographs so that his name appeared only on the front.

Plate 21: 'Market Harborough Town' football team, 1894. (G. Speight)
[LEIMH 100.1983.1312]

Other Studios

Apart from the photographers already described, there were several others who remained in the town for only a short time and who appear to have worked exclusively on portrait work.

The earliest of these was Charles Jacomb, who worked in the town between 1879 and 1881. He is mentioned in a report of court proceedings in the *Market Harborough Advertiser* for the 28 October 1879, when he was jailed for three weeks for damaging a tree. He lived and worked from a house in Coventry Road. The 1881 census shows that he was born in Exeter around 1846, and in 1872 had been living in London. It is not known exactly when he came to Harborough nor indeed when he left. No examples of his work have been found.

A succession of photographers worked from the Bridge House studio. In December 1886 John Dillon Trengove took over from Nichols and remained until March 1891 (*Market Harborough Advertiser*, 21 December 1886). Alexander J. Smith, a Canadian, took over from Trengove, but by December 1892 he had been succeeded by a Mr C. Wallis (*Market Harborough Advertiser*, 3 March 1891). Apart from a single carte-de-visite of Braybrooke church by Smith, only portraits by these photographers survive.

The Rembrandt studio of F.E. Vipond and Company was operating from St Mary's Road in November 1887, when an advertisement appeared in the *Market Harborough Advertiser* for an apprentice. One cabinet portrait and one carte-de-visite have been found from this studio. It has not been possible to determine the exact location of the studio nor the length of time it operated.

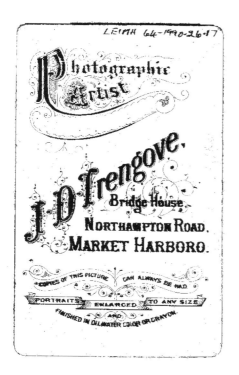

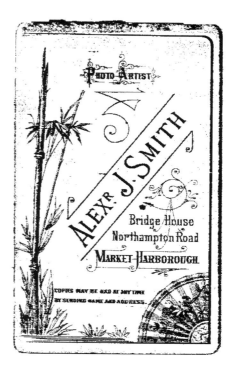

A further studio was opened at No. 13 Patrick Street in 1896 by William S. Smith, who described himself as an artist and landscape photographer. He did, however, undertake portraiture and also offered a picture framing service. His name is not found in any of the commercial directories and it seems likely he only remained in business for a short time. Only one of his photographs has been found and this shows the interior of the swimming pool at its opening (*Market Harborough Advertiser* supplement, 31 July 1896).

Outside Market Harborough, James Main advertised his studio in Hallaton in Kelly's *Leicestershire Directory* of 1876 and Wright's *Leicestershire Directory* of 1880. A James Smeeton had a studio in Kibworth Harcourt between 1870 and 1884. However, nothing further is known about these two individuals, as no census entries and no photographs have been found.

There remains a body of photographs which date from the 1880s and 1890s but cannot be attributed to any of the photographers discussed above. A few are clearly the work of studios elsewhere, while others may be of local origin. Some may be the work of amateurs, while other items could be the work of itinerant photographers. The tradition of travelling photographers, who stayed no more than a few days in any one town or village, was established by Nichols' time and continued well into the twentieth century.

Plate 22: The Revd William Law,
c. 1895. (John Knight Law)
[LEIMH 1.1990.173]

Plate 23: Gulliver Speight, 1933. (Photographer unknown) [Mike Brown]
Speight was a very keen and successful amateur rose grower.

THE PHOTOGRAPHS

What follows is a visual tour around Victorian Market Harborough and its surrounding villages in the company of the photographers discussed in Section Two. Starting in the town, the photographic perambulation begins on the Square and moves north up the western side of the High Street and then back down the eastern frontage. After a visit to Church Square and Adam and Eve Street, there are views along St Mary's Road, followed by pictures of the southern and western approaches to the town along the Northampton and the Coventry Roads. The tour of the villages begins to the south-west of the town, at East Farndon. From here a roughly clockwise route is followed, ending at Great Oxendon.

Only a few of the photographs are dated. For the majority a date has been estimated using various contemporary sources. The working dates of the individual photographers provides a basic starting point, but this has been augmented using datable information found in the images themselves. The two most important are fashion details and the names of commercial occupiers on the signboards of buildings.

The caption to each photograph includes a reference to the location of the original. As noted above, the majority are to be found in the collection of the

Harborough Museum (references prefaced by LEIMH), but other repositories include the Leicestershire Record Office (LRO), Northamptonshire Record Office (NRO), and the Local Studies Department of Northamptonshire County Library (NCL).

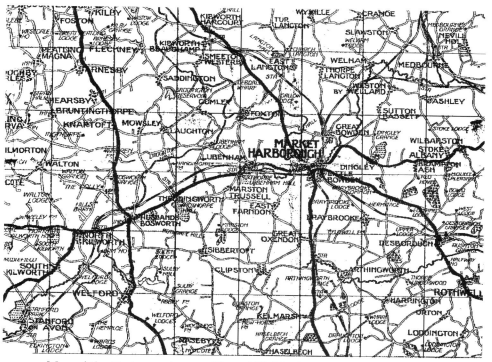

Map of the Harborough area. (From J.W. Harding & Co., *General Map to the District of Market Harborough*, about 1920) [LEIMH 89.1990.7]

Plate 24: The Square, Market Harborough, looking north up the High Street, 1855–6. (W. Law) [LEIMH 100.1983.2491]

Plate 25: The Square, Market Harborough, looking north up the High Street, 1855–6. (W. Law) [LEIMH 100.1983.2487]

Plate 26: The Square, Market Harborough, looking north up the High
Street, 1856. (W Law) [LEIMH 100.1983.2000]

These three photographs are all from waxed paper negatives and at first
glance appear virtually identical, but a closer inspection reveals they were
in fact taken on three separate occasions. The first can be identified as the
earliest from the scaffolding on the building on the western side of the
High Street. This scaffolding was used when a second storey was added
to the present No. 5. In the other photographs there is no scaffolding, but
there is a second storey. The second photo shows the same view but from
a slightly different angle so as to exclude the gas lamp-standard which
stood in the Square. The third includes people, an unusual feature in
Law's topographical work. The relatively long exposure time used in this
photograph is indicated by the blurred image of a child, firstly near the
pump and again by the street lamp. Although the three images are not
dated, an examination of local commercial directories shows that Thomas
Green established his business in 1855, and it is known that in 1856 the
Leicestershire Banking Company rebuilt No. 14 High Street, the building
with the scaffolding (note the extra chimneys in the third view). From this
information we know that the pictures opposite were taken between 1855
and 1856, while that above is slightly later.

Plate 27: The Square, Market Harborough, looking east, 1881. (John Burton and Sons of Leicester) [LEIMH 111.1985.4] This was taken in 1881 when Robert and William Henry Symington rebuilt their factory in Factory Lane. The scaffolding used in the rebuilding can be seen on the extreme left, over the roof of Shindler's, the drapers.

Plate 28: The Square, from Northampton Road, *c.* 1890. (? G. Speight) [LEIMH 87.1985.9 (part)] The entry of Coventry Road on the far side of the Square is not obvious here, partly because of the camera angle and partly because of the narrow end of the road which remained until 1892. In this year the building with the dormer window was demolished to improve and widen this junction.

Plate 29: Market day in the Square, between 1892 and 1895. (? G. Speight) [LEIMH 100.1983.1342] This photograph can be dated to after 1892, when the junction with Coventry Road was improved and the de Capel Brooke memorial fountain was erected in the centre of the Square. It cannot be later than 1895, when Hilton's Booteries took over occupation of No. 28 The Square from Thomas Dunkley. The picture is attributed to Gulliver Speight because of its elevated viewpoint. From 1894 Speight occupied No. 5 The Square; he may well have taken this photograph from the window of his studio.

Plate 30: East side of the Square, *c.* 1865. (J.P. Jennings) [LEIMH 90.1986.6]

Plate 31: East side of the Square, *c.* 1865. (J.P. Jennings) [LEIMH 51.1989.62]

Plate 32: East side of the Square, *c.* 1865. (J.P. Jennings) [LEIMH 93.1983.12]

These three plates show a drapers shop on the site now occupied by Nos 22–4 The Square. George Emery moved to these premises in about 1864 and remained in business there until his death in 1894. These may well have been commissioned by Mr Emery to advertise his business. The first two are in carte-de-visite format, the third was taken using a different camera with a slightly wider angle lens and includes Nos 26 and 20 The Square.

Plate 33: East side of the Square, *c.* 1875. (Photographer unknown) [LEIMH 55.1991.2] This shop lay to the south of Emery's drapery (see plates 27–9); today the site is occupied by No. 20 The Square. George Veasey, a cabinet maker, occupied this shop from before 1870 and took over a boot and shoe business in the right hand shop in 1874. In 1881 he changed the shop-fronts, thus making this date the latest possible for the photograph. However, the best clues to the date come from an examination of the census returns for 1871. These show that George Veasey was 27 years old with a wife and two sons aged 2 and 2 weeks. From the ages of the children in the photograph, a date of about 1875 would seem most likely, the younger child still being in skirts and so below the age of 6 or 7 years old.

Plates 34 and 35: The garden of Welland House, the south side of the Square, Market Harborough, 1860s and 1880s. (Photographer unknown and G.A. Nichols) [both LRO DE 3736 (part)] Most of this garden is now occupied by the Garden of Remembrance. The top plate shows the friends and relations of William Andrews, a solicitor. The bottom plate shows the same garden twenty years later when it belonged to Mr George Staynes, the owner of the nearby tannery.

Plate 36: Looking north-east up the High Street at St Dionysius' church, between 1864 and 1868. (J.P. Jennings) [LEIMH 99.1987.323] This is an early view of the church, taken between 1863, when Charles Hatwood, hairdresser and toyseller, moved into the corner shop of Church Square and High Street, and 1868 when the Old Grammar School was restored.

Plate 37: The interior of St Dionysius' church, early 1860s. (J.P. Jennings) [LEIMH 7.1991] This interior shows the elaborate illuminated script of the Ten Commandments, which adorned the walls of the church, and the alabaster pulpit (by William Smith of London) erected in 1860.

Plate 38: The Market Harborough April Fair on the lower High Street,
1860. (W.J. Jennings) [LEIMH A.6331] This photograph must have been
taken before 1861 because the pavements in the High Street had been
flagged by then. For Jennings this was an ambitious subject, the time
required for exposure making some blurring inevitable. Plate 39 shows
exactly the same elevated view of the High Street as in the previous
photograph. The most striking contrast between the two, however, is the
quality of the image. The 'instantaneous' process adopted by Gulliver
Speight meant no difficulties with moving people. This photograph was
probably taken about 1890, but was used in several publications in the
1890s and early 1900s and was each time given a different date.

Plate 39: The Market Harborough April Fair on the lower High Street, 1890. (G. Speight) [LEIMH 100.1983.1133]

Plate 40: West side of the High Street, *c.* 1895. (Photographer unknown) [LEIMH 124.1986] This shop was occupied by Emmanuel Plowman, a nurseryman. He began his business with a market stall before opening a shop in Church Street in 1874. In 1877 he moved to this property in the High Street. The Plowman family continued in business in these premises until the 1970s.

Plate 41: The west side of the lower High Street, *c.* 1890. (? G. Speight) [LEIMH 99.1987.380] This is another view published in the 1892 trade guide to the town. It shows the Talbot public house before the second storey was removed. Most of the buildings between the Talbot and the Three Swans have been rebuilt since this photograph was taken.

Plate 42: Church's, High Street, 1890s. (Photographer unknown) [LEIMH 1.1990.162] This building, erected in 1883, occupied the site of the present No. 10 High Street. The corn merchant business of Henry Church and Son was located here from the 1850s until the 1950s.

Plate 43: West side of the lower High Street, between 1875 and 1880. (E.H. Speight) [LEIMH 100.1983.1104] It is often difficult to determine a date for photographs portraying long-term businesses such as Goward's. However, this image can be dated to E.H. Speight's work in the town.

Plate 44: Goward's grocery, High Street, 1892. (? G. Speight) [LEIMH 51.1987.6 (part)] The site of this shop is now occupied by No. 18 High Street. Thomas Goward established this business in 1810 and it was continued by his son until the early years of this century. The bearded gentleman in this photograph is Thomas Goward junior. This image appears in the 1892 trade guide.

Plate 45: Looking north up the High Street, between 1854 and 1861. (W. Jennings) [LEIMH 100.1983.1186] To the left can be seen the Three Swans Inn, and on the right the Town Hall. This photograph can be dated to between 1854, when John West, a hairdresser, moved into the shop to the north of the Three Swans (No. 23 High Street – note the barber's pole on the front of the shop), and 1861, when the pavements were flagged. This print is made from a wet collodion plate.

Plate 46: The High Street from the Three Swans Inn, *c.* 1890. (G. Speight) [LEIMH 99.1987.378] John West's barber's pole can still be seen outside No. 23 High Street.

Plate 47: Coach and Horses public house, west side of High Street, *c.* 1900. (G. Speight) [LEIMH 100.1983.1188] This pub was demolished in 1901 to make way for Abbey Street. The photograph was taken shortly before demolition.

Plates 48 and 49: Ridley's Yard (now Abbey Street), *c.* 1900. (G. Speight) [LEIMH 32.1990.20 and LEIMH 100.1983.1273] Two views of Ridley's Yard taken in about 1900 just before the houses were demolished and Abbey Street was built. The open window of the house in the centre of the lower view is seen again above. Such yards were developed in the eighteenth century on the rear of the long, thin properties which were laid out either side of the High Street when the town was established in the twelfth century.

Plate 50: The Corn Exchange and Manor House, west side of the High Street, between 1875 and 1880. (E.H. Speight) [LEIMH 100.1983.1107] The Corn Exchange, on the left, was built in 1858 to provide offices for a number of businesses along with the Assembly Room, a venue for various social functions. It was renovated in 1903 and then replaced totally by the present Golden Wonder offices in the 1960s. At the time of this photograph the Manor House was still a private residence in the occupation of Mr Ben Pulver, a farmer. The posts and chains along the edge of the road were intended to keep cattle away from the footpaths on market day.

Plate 51: The interior of the Corn Exchange, between 1861 and 1870. (J.P. Jennings) [LEIMH 100.1983.1178] This is an unusual early view of a building's interior. This photograph was probably a commissioned piece, but unfortunately it is not known what event is taking place.

Plates 52 and 53: The west side of the upper High Street, *c.* 1898.
(G. Speight) [both LEIMH 87.1985.9 (part)] The shadowy image in the
picture above was caused by someone walking across the street while the
photograph was being taken. The second plate shows the Angel Hotel, a
coaching inn developed in the late eighteenth century.

Plate 54: The upper High Street, late 1850s. (W. Law) [LEIMH 100.1983.2489] The upper High Street was a popular subject with photographers from William Law onwards. Law's waxed paper negative from the mid-1850s was taken from an upper window of the Town Hall. Shadows cast from the west suggest it was taken early in the afternoon, while the piles of dung in the street suggest a Tuesday livestock market had been held earlier in the day. Plate 50 can be attributed to the earlier date of the two because it shows the double-fronted house on the right (today's No. 51 High Street) without the bay window façade. Plate 51 can be dated to between 1897, when a shop-front was added to the Manor Buildings, and 1903, when livestock were no longer sold in the street.

Plate 55: The upper High Street, between 1888 and 1891. (G. Speight)
[LEIMH 50.1987]

Plate 56: The upper High Street, between 1897 and 1903. (G. Speight)
[LEIMH 99.1987.261]

Plate 57: High Elms Park, Market Harborough, about 1898. (G. Speight) [LEIMH 87.1985.9 (part)] This photograph was taken for a supplement to the *Estates Gazette* for March 1898. It is something of a mystery, as no exact location for High Elms Park has been found. Most probably it was what was later to become the grounds of Park House, originally called Elm Park.

Plate 58: Looking south down Leicester Road into Market Harborough, *c.* 1892. (G. Speight) [LEIMH 99.1987.624] The wall on the left marks the boundary of Brooke House, then called the Elms and the home of the de Capel Brooke family.

Plates 59 and 60: Exterior and interior of the Congregational church, Market Harborough, 1860s and 1880s. (J.P. Jennings and G.A. Nichols) [LEIMH 1.1990.234 and LEIMH 1.1990.232] This church was built in 1844 on the site of a complex of buildings which had been used for Independent worship since 1694. The architect was William Flint of Leicester. Gas lighting replaced the candelabra in 1894.

Plate 61: Looking south-east down the upper High Street, probably 1890s.
(? G. Speight) [LEIMH 100.1983.2500] The topographical detail in this
photograph only allows a wide date range – between 1877, when George
Limbird took over the Angel Hotel on the right, and 1901, when Abbey
Street was built on the site of several buildings to the right of the Town
Hall. However, the finish on this print is identical to that of Speight's
known work. If this is the case, the picture may be dated to the last
decade of the nineteenth century.

Plate 62: The Town Hall, *c.* 1892. (? G. Speight) [LEIMH 87.1985.9 (part)]
This view of the Town Hall from the north appeared in the 1892 trade
guide. On the right can be seen the Coach and Horses inn demolished in
1901 to make way for Abbey Street.

Plate 63: A group of shops on the eastern side of the upper High Street, between 1864 and 1873. (Jennings) [LEIMH 100.1983.1152] This block of shops was built in 1845 by the Town Estate, and at the time of this photograph was occupied by John Patrick, a butcher, Ben Rolleston, a baker, William Allen, a jeweller, and Edward Skinner, a draper. The photograph was taken after 1864, when Edward Skinner moved his business from Adam and Eve Street, but before 1873 when Ben Rolleston retired.

Plate 64: Wilkinson's printers, east side of lower High Street, *c.* 1900. (Photographer unknown) [LEIMH 99.1987.264] This photograph of a shop in everyday use contrasts markedly with the rather posed commemorative pictures of Victorian shops which usually survive (compare plates 72 and 82).

Plate 65: The south-east view of the lower High Street, between 1864 and 1867. (W. Jennings) [LEIMH 100.1983.1176] This view of the High Street can be dated to between 1863, when Charles Hatwood moved to the corner of Church Square, and 1867, when Joseph Collins took over the George Hotel on the extreme right.

Plates 66 and 67: The Old Grammar School, Market Harborough, *c.* 1865 and *c.* 1880. (? Jennings family and E.H. Speight) [LEIMH 92.1983.17 and LEIMH 1.1990.266] This picturesque timber building was erected in 1614 and had its bellcote added in 1789. These two photographs show the school before and after a major refurbishment in 1868. The extension to the rear of the building was added during this restoration.

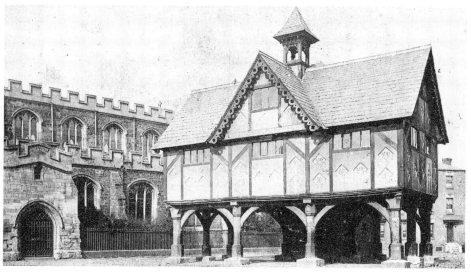

Plate 68: The corner of High Street, looking north-east up the lower High Street, between 1863 and 1868. (? J.P. Jennings) [LEIMH 100.1983.1219] Charles Hatwood and later his son occupied this shop from 1863 until 1909. However, this photograph can be dated to before 1868 by comparing the building in front of the Town Hall with the same building on plate 36.

Plate 69: The north-eastern view of Church Square, 1870s. (E.H. Speight) [LEIMH 100.1983.1098] The third shop on the left was occupied by the Market Harborough Industrial Co-operative Society. This had been set up in Church Square in 1862 but moved to larger premises on the lower High Street in 1866, before returning to Church Square in the 1870s.

Plate 70: Looking north up Church Street, between 1864 and 1870. (J.P. Jennings) [LEIMH 51.1989.61] This is an unusual view of Church Street, not often photographed because of the difficult angles. Aldwinkle's ironmongers shop can be seen on the right and the Rose and Crown inn on the left. The thatched cottages at the far end of the right hand side of the street were demolished in 1894 when the Nag's Head pub was rebuilt.

Plate 71: Eastern corner of Church Street and Church Square, between 1859 and 1861. (? W. Jennings) [LEIMH 99.1989.198] This view was taken before the pavements were flagged in 1861, but after John Smith, a butcher, bought the corner property in 1859. John Smith occupied this site until 1879. A haberdashery shop appears to be to the left of the butcher. Next to this is William Eland, a printer and stationer responsible for founding the town's first newspaper, the *Market Harborough Advertiser* in 1854.

Plate 72: North-east corner of Church Square, between 1881 and 1897. (Photographer unknown) [LEIMH 100.1983.1225] This is a standard format for shop photographs later in the century. The large arrays of produce usually recorded in these pictures were certainly stage-managed, but the day of the photographer's visit probably coincided with special sales at Easter or Christmas, which would account for the large stock. This building was demolished in 1936 when Roman Way was constructed.

Plate 73: North-eastern corner of Church Square and Church Gate, between 1878 and 1888. (Photographer unknown) [LEIMH A.6376] This building and its neighbours were demolished in 1888.

Plate 74: Looking east down Church Gate (now Adam and Eve Street), 1888. (G. Speight) [LEIMH 51.1989.28] This side of Church Gate was demolished in 1888 for the site of the 'new side' of the R. & W.H. Symington factory. The 'old side' was to the right of the photograph in Factory Lane. The man on the extreme left has been identified as Charles Wilford, a part-time fireman.

Plate 75: Looking south down Factory Lane, *c.* 1880. (F.W. Broadhead)
[LRO DE 2262.160.1] On the left is the 'old side' of the R. & W.H.
Symington corset factory, a former worsted and carpet factory taken over
in the 1850s. Outside the entrance are perambulators used by outworkers
to transport garments from home to the factory.

Plates 76 and 77: North side of Church Gate, 1888. (? G. Speight) [LRO DE 2262.150–151] These two plates show the properties along Church Gate being demolished in 1888 in preparation for the building of R. & W.H. Symington's second corset factory.

Plate 77

Plate 78: St Dionysius' church from Church Gate, 1867. (W. Jennings)
[NRO NAS 47.17] This photograph was taken just before the renovation
of the Old Grammar School building on the left. On the right is a house
and shop occupied by Henry White, who traded as the unlikely combina-
tion of greengrocer and brickmaker. In the centre of Church Square is a
gas lamp-post with a water pump at its base.

Plates 79 and 80: Looking west into Church Square from Church Gate, 1860s and 1888. (J.P. Jennings and ? G. Speight) [LEIMH 111.1985.2 and LEIMH 51.1989.23] In the top picture the man wearing the apron on the right hand side of the photograph is John Jarvis, a shoemaker, who kept the shop on the extreme right between 1861 and 1867. John Jarvis was born in Desborough, but spent most of his working life in Harborough, previously occupying shops in Church Street and St Mary's Road. The lower photograph was taken shortly before the site was cleared in 1888. By this time, John Jarvis' shop is boarded up.

Plate 81: Looking north up Adam and Eve Street, 1877. (E.H. Speight) [LEIMH 100.1983.1100] At the far end of the right hand row can be seen the sign of Walter Symington's grocery shop, established in 1877. In 1878 he went into partnership with George Thwaites. The business prospered and became one of the leading shops in the town during the early twentieth century.

Plate 82: West side of Adam and Eve Street, *c*. 1895. (Photographer unknown) [LEIMH 1.1991.301] This publicity photograph was probably commissioned by Mr Garner, the tall gentleman in the doorway, during the Christmas season (note the holly decorating the carcasses).

Plate 83: The Peacock, between 1879 and 1897. (? G. Speight) [LEIMH 119.1984]. Commercial details date this photograph between 1879, when James Wallis established his posting business in the Peacock yard, and 1897, when the business was removed to another part of St Mary's Road.

Plate 84: Allsop's stonemasons yard, south side of St Mary's Road, between 1892 and 1901. (G. Speight) [LEIMH 100.1983.1258] William Allsop, monumental mason, occupied this builder's yard from 1892 until 1901, when the site was developed for the present post office building. Note the chimney pots stored on the wooden framework.

Plate 85: South side of St Mary's Road, *c*. 1892. (G. Speight) [LEIMH 100.1983.1311] The buildings in this photograph were demolished in 1901 to make way for the present No.10 St Mary's Road. This photograph was probably taken in 1892, by which date George Fairbrother, a basketmaker, had moved to the first of the three-storey cottages, but John Newcombe had not yet moved into the property shown in the picture below.

Plate 86: North side of St Mary's Road, *c*. 1893. (G. Speight) [LEIMH 100.1983.1314] John Newcombe took over these premises in 1893 when Mr E.T. Garner, a grocer, went bankrupt. This building of 1857 has since been replaced by the present No. 27 St Mary's Road.

Plate 87: The Windmill, Mill Hill, 1895. (G. Speight) [LEIMH 100.1983.1302] In Victorian times almost every town and village had its own windmill. Despite the building of the steam mills further along St Mary's Road in 1857 (see plate 90) this post-mill operated until the final years of the nineteenth century. In this photograph the miller, John Harry Smith, is seated on the cart with his younger brother. The Smith family operated this mill from the early 1800s.

Plates 88 and 89: The north side of St Mary's Road, late 1870s. (E.H. Speight) [LEIMH 100.1983.1108 and LEIMH 100.1983.1101] Most of the buildings shown here have been replaced. They are of varied scale and date, typical of the early ribbon development which took place along this eastern route out of the town from the late eighteenth century onwards.

Plate 90: The steam mills, the south-east end of St Mary's Road, 1861.
(Photographer unknown) [LEIMH 51.1989.46] This photograph shows the
town's first steam-driven corn mill, erected in 1857. In the background is
the Rugby to Stamford railway. The wide angle of the camera lens suggests a much greater distance between the two than actually existed. On
the left can be seen the bridge which was the original crossing point of the
River Welland for the London Road. This was moved to its present position when the railway was built. The mottled appearance of the photograph is caused by the fibres of the paper on the original print showing
through. Some touching up has been undertaken on the chimney and roof
of the steam mills to give the very dark outline.

Plate 91: A locomotive at Market Harborough railway station, *c.* 1860. (W. Jennings) [LEIMH 100.1983.1427] This early passenger train was travelling from Peterborough to Rugby. The engine is an LNWR Southern Division 2–2–2, built in 1848 by Sharp Brothers. The man in the top hat is probably George Henry Rich, the stationmaster, and the man beside him the engine-driver.

Plates 92, 93 and 94: The former Little Bowden rectory, *c*. 1865. (Jennings family) [LEIMH 92.1983.35, LEIMH 92.1983.36 and LEIMH 92.1983.37] This set of three cartes-de-visite depicts the former rectory of Little Bowden. This interesting building dates from 1627 and is now a private house. The photograph above shows the front of the building looking much as it does today. The woman and girl on show below are wearing clothes fashionable in the early 1860s.

Plate 94: The rear garden of Little Bowden rectory as seen from what is now Little Bowden Bowls Club, *c.* 1865. (Jennings family).

Plate 95: Little Bowden church, from the north-east, between 1861 and 1868. (Jennings family) [LEIMH 100.1983.1351] This photograph shows labourers scything the grass in the churchyard. An examination of the memorial stones in the churchyard reveals a stone dated 1868 which does not appear in the photograph so presumably the photograph was taken before that date.

Plate 96: A Royal Jubilee tea at Little Bowden, 1887. (Photographer unknown) [LEIMH 100.1983.3053] Little Bowden's celebration of Queen Victoria's Golden Jubilee in 1887. The event took place in Mr West's Home Close, a field behind Rectory Lane and adjacent to the Manor House.

Plate 97: Little Bowden steam mills, looking north-west, *c.* 1870.
(Photographer unknown) [LEIMH 99.1983.474] William Symington established this factory to roast coffee and process pea flour some time before
1850. In the foreground runs Springfield Street, then called Billy Boys
Lane. This photograph was taken before 1871, when a row of cottages was
built to the east of the range of buildings seen in the picture. The factory
frontage was rebuilt in 1881.

Plates 98 and 99: Market Harborough municipal swimming pool, Northampton Road, 1896. (G. Speight and William S. Smith) [LEIMH 36.1987.3] On 6 October 1896 the *Market Harborough Advertiser* commemorated the opening of the town's first swimming pool with a special supplement. This included these two photographs.

Plate 100: The north side of Coventry Road, looking east towards the Square, between 1875 and 1878. (E.H. Speight) [LEIMH 100.1983.1103] These houses were built in 1866 by Thomas Palmer, whose sign is seen on the wall of the left hand house. He remained in business here until 1878.

Plate 101: Bowling Green Place, looking east, about 1855. (W. Law)
[LEIMH 100.1983.2490] This unusual view was taken from the corner of
Fairfield Road and School Lane. The cottages on the right were known as
Bowling Green Place.

Plate 102: The south side of Coventry Road, looking east towards the Square, between 1875 and 1881. (E.H. Speight) [LEIMH 135.1986.3] Most of these buildings were demolished for a road widening scheme carried out in 1892. The seemingly transparent box on the left hand pavement in front of the man with the broom resulted from its being placed there half way through the long exposure of the negative.

Plate 103: The south side of Coventry Road, looking south-east, between 1875 and 1880. (E.H. Speight) [LEIMH 100.1983.1106] The group of houses seen here was known as Western Terrace. Beyond is the town's vicarage, built in 1875. This was demolished in 1991 for the site of the health centre.

Plates 104 and 105: The former Congregational manse, Coventry Road, *c.* 1880. (F.W. Broadhead) [LEIMH 1.1990.265 and LEIMH 1.1990.272] These front and rear views show the purpose-built manse of the minister of the town's Congregational church which was erected in 1874. The property was sold to private owners in 1931.

Plate 106: The Willows, Coventry Road, between 1875 and 1880. (E.H. Speight) [LEIMH 100.1983.1105] At this time Thomas Scarborough lived in The Willows, with his wife and six children. Scarborough ran a haberdashery business in Church Street for many years.

Plate 107: Looking north down Harborough Road, East Farndon, 1862. (W. Law) [LEIMH 100.1983.3052] Unfortunately, this old print from a glass plate is badly damaged. This view shows the junction of the main road through the village with the road leading to Marston Trussell. Thatched cob walls, seen on both sides of the road, were typical of this area at this time.

Plates 108 and 109: Looking north to the church and school, Sibbertoft, about 1855 and 1862. (W. Law) These photographs show Sibbertoft church and village school. In plate 108 the church is seen before restoration, while in plate 109 restoration is in progress with the porch and chancel roof removed. The larger photograph is from a waxed paper negative, and the smaller is from a collodion plate.

Plate 109: Looking north to the church and school, Sibbertoft, 1862. (W. Law)

Plate 110: Naseby Road, Sibbertoft, *c.* 1875. (W. Law) [LEIMH 54.1987.1]
This site is now occupied by a group of council houses.

Plates 111 and 112: Looking south and north along Church Street, Sibbertoft, *c.* 1880. (W. Law) [LEIMH 100.1983.1390 and LEIMH 54.1987.3] The white cottage with its gable end on the street is an inn which changed its name from The Swan to The Old Swan in the mid-1870s. However, by 1884 it had closed.

Plate 113: Clipston church, 1868. (W. Jennings) [NRO NAS 47.12] An intriguing question is posed in this photograph by the woman sitting in the churchyard. Is she mourning a loved one or was the photographer just using her to give his picture a human focus?

Plate 114: Kelmarsh church from the north, about 1861. (W. Jennings)
[NRO NAS 48.38] Here we see the church before the restoration of 1874.

Plate 115: Looking north into Naseby village, 1855. (W. Law) [LEIMH 100.1983.2482] This photograph shows Naseby as it was before much of the village was rebuilt at the end of the nineteenth century.

Plate 116: Looking east towards the church, Naseby, 1860s. (W. Law) [NRO P1126] This picture shows the new spire on the church, which was completed in 1859.

Plate 117: The south side of Welford church, *c*. 1856. (W. Law) [LEIMH 100.1983.2074] The man in the top hat is believed to be Henry Ferraby at the grave of his father, the Revd John Ferraby, who was vicar of Welford for twenty-four years. The children seated by the porch are probably Henry Ferraby's two daughters.

Plate 118: South Kilworth church, 1867. (? W. Jennings) [LEIMH 123.1985.3] This photograph was taken just before the restoration of the church in 1868.

Plate 119: Husbands Bosworth School, *c*. 1885. (G.A. Nichols) [LEIMH 51.1989.75] This school was built in 1858 and provided education for children in many of the surrounding villages. In the foreground is Mr Houghton, who was headmaster from its foundation until his death in 1886.

Plates 120 and 121: Looking north-west and south-east along the High Street, Husbands Bosworth, between 1876 and 1886. (John Burton & Son, Leicester, and E.H. Speight) [LEIMH 1.1991.235 and LEIMH 1.1991.115]

Plate 122: Mowsley Road, Husbands Bosworth, between 1877 and 1895. (Photographer unknown) [LEIMH 1.1991.236] John Scrimshire is seen in the centre of this photograph (in an apron) with his family around him. He worked as a tailor in Husbands Bosworth from 1877 until the turn of the century.

Plate 123: Main Street, Husbands Bosworth, 1890s. (Photographer unknown) [LEIMH 1.1992.118] Thomas Henry Porter ran this saddlers business from about 1890 until the 1930s.

Plate 124: Looking east along Main Street, Theddingworth, *c.* 1900. (G. Speight) [LEIMH 4.1990] The school on the right was built in 1844, and this photograph was taken just before an infants' room was added in 1902. Note the pupils peeping over the wall.

Plate 125: Marston Trussell Hall, 1856. (W. Law) [LEIMH 100.1983.2361]
This early photograph of Marston Trussell Hall is dated 1856 and depicts
the west wing which has since been demolished.

Plate 126: Looking east along Main Street, Marston Trussell, 1893. (? W. Law) [LEIMH 100.1983.3055] This photograph looks towards the school and the Sun Inn from outside the hall stables. Some of the buildings on the right were demolished when the new road to Sibbertoft and East Farndon was built following the creation of the lake by the squire, Mr Ewins Bennett.

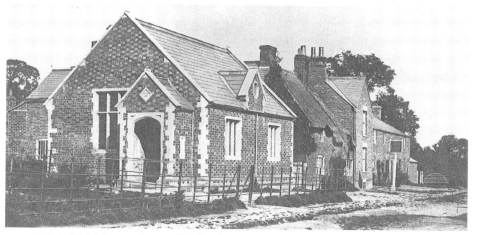

Plate 127: Marston Trussell School, 1875. (W. Law) [LEIMH 100.1983.2066] This school was established in 1852 on the initiative of the Revd William Law, and finally erected by 1857. The thatched cottage beyond the school was used as accommodation for the staff.

Plates 128 and 129: The Coach and Horses Inn, Lubenham, *c.* 1865 and 1883. (W. Jennings and G. Nichols) [LEIMH A.6362 and LEIMH 99.1987.639] The earlier of these photographs shows the inn before its renovation in the early 1870s, when it changed its name from The Swan. The image can be attributed to Jennings from its composition and format. The later photo has been dated by reference to the parade of Triumph Lodge No. 179 of the village Oddfellows Friendly Society outside the inn.

Plate 130: The Old Hall, Lubenham, early 1860s. (W. Law) [LEIMH 1.1991.249] The print of this photograph was made by Law in 1893, although the plate was probably made about thirty years before.

Plate 131: Looking north to Lubenham church, 1856. (W. Law) [LEIMH 100.1983.2077] This shows Lubenham church on 4 August 1856. The farm-house to the left of the picture was rebuilt in 1862 to create today's Tower House.

Plate 132: Interior of the nave of Lubenham church, *c.* 1896. (Photographer unknown) [LEIMH 1.1991.244] An interior view of the church showing the box pews and gallery of 1812 (the latter was removed in about 1897).

Plate 133: Black Horse Inn, Foxton, 1870. (Photographer unknown) [LRO DE 3736 (part)] The small building to the left of the inn was the brewhouse, where the beer was made. The inn was rebuilt in 1900.

Plate 134: Bottom of Foxton locks, between 1860 and 1890. (W. Law) [LEIMH 100.1983.2351] Cottages at the bottom of Foxton locks photographed by William Law. The building in the centre of the picture is now the Bridge 61 public house.

Plate 135: Looking up Foxton locks, *c.* 1898. (Photographer unknown) [LEIMH 99.1987.156] This flight of locks was constructed between 1810 and 1814 to link the Trent and Soar river navigations with the London to Birmingham canal system. In the top left hand corner can be seen the inclined plane barge lift under construction.

Plates 136, 137 and 138: Constructing the Foxton inclined plane barge lift, between 1898 and 1900. (? Thomas Millner) [LEIMH A.6796, A.6802, and A.6801] This lift was designed to reduce the time taken to travel the Foxton incline. The journey took about an hour using the locks, but only eight minutes on the barge lift. The lift was designed by Gordon Thomas of the Grand Junction Canal Company and was a considerable feat of engineering design and construction. He and his wife are inspecting the construction in plate 138. However it was not a commercial success and ceased operation in 1910, being dismantled in 1928. These photographs were possibly taken by Thomas Millner, Area Manager for the Grand Junction Canal Co. at Blisworth.

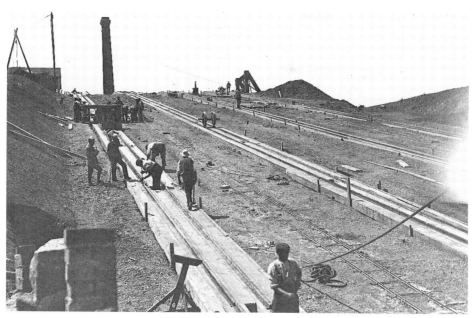

Plate 137

Plate 138

Plates 139 and 140: Lock 18, Kibworth, before and after reconstruction, 1896. (Photographer unknown) [LEIMH A.6451 and A.6452] An inscription on the bottom of plate 135 identifies the location as Lock 24, but close inspection of the canal shows this is incorrect.

Plate 141: Queen Victoria's Diamond Jubilee celebrations at the Bank, Kibworth Beauchamp, 1897. (Photographer unknown) [LRO DE 1863.395] It is surprising that no other Victorian photographs of Kibworth are known.

Plate 142: The village green, Church Langton, between 1884 and 1892.
(E. Griffiths, Leicester) [LEIMH 1.1991.165]

Plate 143: The Green, Great Bowden, 1860s. (W. Jennings) [LEIMH
90.1984.9] This shows the north-west side of the Green. On the left is Main
Street, and on the right Sutton Road.

Plate 144: The Green, Great Bowden, 1860s. (? W. Jennings) [LEIMH 90.1984.10] This shows the south-western corner of the Green from the signpost seen in the previous picture.

Plate 145: Dingley Road, Great Bowden, 1860s. (? W. Jennings) [LEIMH 90.1984.8] On the left is the village's National School which was built in 1839.

Plate 146: Great Bowden church, 1861. (W. Jennings) [LEIMH 100.1983.3054]

Plates 147 and 148: The interior of Great Bowden church, *c*. 1885.
(G. Nichols) [LEIMH 90.1984.6 and LEIMH 90.1984.5] These two views
show the furnishings of the church before the restoration of 1888. The
aesthetics of the nave are not helped by the prominent flue of the stove!

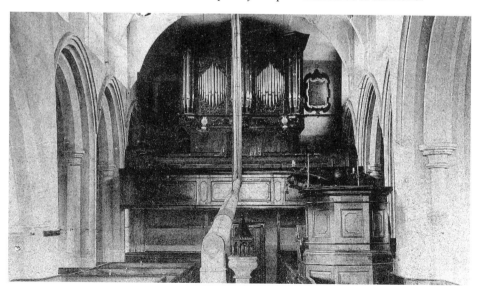

Plate 149: Chancel and south side of Sutton Bassett church during restoration, 1861. (W. Jennings) [NRO NAS 48.76] This and the following three photos were taken by Jennings for the Architectural Society of the Archdeanery of Northampton.

Plate 150: North side of Sutton Bassett during restoration, 1861. (W. Jennings) [NRO NAS 48.77] Victorian church restorations often involved complete rebuilding, and such a scheme had been proposed here. However, public opposition resulted in far less radical work, although even this seems drastic by today's standards.

Plate 151: Workmen taking a break on the south side of Sutton Bassett church during restoration, 1861. (W. Jennings) [NRO NAS 48.78]

Plate 152: The south side of Sutton Bassett church after restoration, 1867. (W. Jennings) [NRO NAS 47.33]

Plate 153: The Green, Weston by Welland, late nineteenth century.
(Photographer unknown) [LEIMH 1.1990.33] This anonymous carte-de-
visite could have been taken anytime between 1860 and 1900. There is no
photographer's mark or costume detail to help date this photograph.

Plate 154: The south side of Weston by Welland church, 1865.
(W. Jennings) [NRO NAS 47.35] This was taken just after the restoration
of 1863–5.

Plate 155: The Independent chapel, Ashley, early 1890s. (Photographer unknown) [LEIMH 1.1992.35] The minister, the Revd Mr Butler, stands with his family outside his cottage manse and adjoining chapel. Both were built sometime before 1706. The chapel was renovated in 1892, before this was taken.

Plates 156 and 157: Exterior and interior of Wilbarston church, *c*. 1865.
(? W. Jennings) [LEIMH 90.1985.1 and LEIMH 90.1985.2] These two views
of Wilbarston church were taken before the restoration of 1884.

Plate 158: Braybrooke church from the south, *c.* 1892. (Alexander J. Smith) [NCL G1697] A rare photograph by Alexander Smith, who had a photographic studio in Market Harborough only from March 1891 until the end of 1892.

Plate 159: Garden of the rectory at Braybrooke, 1870s. (W. Daynes of Rugby) [LEIMH 1.1992.123] This shows the Revd Mr Field and his family.

Plate 160: The south side of Artingworth church, 1861. (W. Jennings) [NRO NAS 48.1] This photograph shows the design of the church before the restoration of 1872.

Plate 161: The George Inn, Great Oxendon, *c*. 1895. (Photographer unknown) [LEIMH 1.1991.51] Some of the occupants, members of the Russell family, stand by the door.

Plate 162: Constructing a railway tunnel at Great Oxendon, 1856. (W. Law) [LEIMH 100.1983.2494] This windlass was probably used for the construction of the Great Oxendon tunnel for the LNWR line from Market Harborough to Northampton which opened in February 1859. Note the traces for the horses on the right of the picture.

PICTURE CREDITS

C. Allington • R. Arnold • M. Barlow • M. Beech
M. Bradley • I.R. Broughton • M. Brown • Mr Bull
J. and M. Burton • the late J. Carter • A. Cornwall
the late J.C. Davies • M. Gamble • B. Giggins
E.A. Gilbert • R. Hart • B. and P. Heathcote
Husbands Bosworth Historical Society • B. Johnson
Lincolnshire Museums Service (Stamford)
London Borough of Croydon Library
the late J. March • Market Harborough Historical
Society • M. Marjoram • National Railway Museum,
York • Northamptonshire County Libraries
Northamptonshire Record Office • G. Pickering
G. Pitcher • H. Porter • K. Reynolds • C. Raunce
M. Salter • D. and A. Smith • T.R. Smith • W. Smith
S. Southwell • C. Spanton • A. Stewart • G. Tack
P. Thurfield • Warwickshire County Libraries (Rugby)
A. Watts • E. Westaway • M. Westaway • M. Wilford
G.W. Williams • R. Wright